Ann Langton   An anthology of football verse from Homer to Gazza.

First published in 2006
Northwest Regional Development
Agency, PO Box 37,
Renaissance House, Warrington
WA1 1XB.

SAVED
An anthology of football verse
©2006
Northwest Regional Development
Agency.

I

All rights reserved.

No part of this publication may
be reproduced, stored in
a retrieval system or transmitted
in any form or by any means,
electrical, mechanical or otherwise,
without first seeking the written
permission of the publishers.

British Library Cataloguing in
Publication Data.

A catalogue record for this book is
available from the British Library.

ISBN 0-955412-70-6

Designed by The Chase

Printed in the UK by Herbert Walker

For Harry and our family

My thanks go to Bryan Gray and Keith Cooper for making an idea happen, to Cicely Herbert for friendly encouragement and expert advice, to Ann Edwards and Mike Hughes for great help, to Keith Wallace for the Workington poems, to Robert Middleton who advised on the selection of French and German poems, to Benoit Hermermann who helped to identify the French verses and to Lionel Hatch and The Chase Creative Consultants who laboured for love.

To all of you: thank you for your patience.

Ann Langton

"To feel poetically about football
is a way to a proper appreciation of life"

PERCY M. YOUNG   FOOTBALL WRITER AND HISTORIAN

kick off

a game of bloody noses

I say - wizard tackle

Your King and Country need You

'ere we go

a funny old game

football invades the world

More than just a game I discovered poetry around the same time that I discovered football: as a schoolboy at Wath-upon-Dearne in Yorkshire in the 1960's. At the time there was no link whatsoever in my mind. The connection was made many years' later when I became Chairman of Preston North End Football Club in 1994 and subsequently helped to create the National Football Museum. I had no ambition to play any part in football. As so often in life, chance played a part. Prince Charles challenged business people to play their part in local communities; I met Ben Casey (a Preston supporter) who suggested Baxi support its local football club; Baxi (a boiler company, I was Chief Executive) acquired Preston North End; I became Chairman and had the idea to create the National Football Museum within Preston's stadium. A further series of encounters led me to Harry Langton, whose collection was the foundation of the Museum. Harry and I shared the view that the Museum should appeal to a wide range of people, and not just football supporters. His collection allowed us to do this: as well as footballs, kit and trophies it contained ceramics, fine art and ephemera of all kinds. The Museum was able to tell the story of football while at the same time appealing to those with other interests. Harry was the inspiration behind the National Football Museum, his wife Ann was the inspiration for this book. Sadly, Harry died before the Museum opened (but he lives on at Deepdale as recordings he made before his death are used in the Museum). Following Harry's death Ann agreed to bring together a collection of football poetry. I offered to help raise the funds necessary. Three people who played an important part in the creation of the National Football Museum helped. Keith Cooper (my first contact at FIFA) arranged critical funding from UEFA and Ben Casey and Lionel Hatch (of The Chase) took on design and production. The creation of this volume has taken much time and effort. The Museum has been a great success: over 100,000 each year make the pilgrimage to Preston, one of the original members of the Football League. I hope that some of the visitors, and others, will read this book and discover yet again that football is more than just a game. Bryan Gray. Founder Chairman, National Football Museum

Poetry and football? An unlikely partnership some may think; one a refined expression of the human mind (Coleridge's 'best words in the best order'), the other a tough, physical challenge to the strength, skills and co-ordination of the human body. But reflect on the disciplines, techniques and practice both demand, and think, too, of the emotions aroused by football games at all levels – the hope and dread, love and hate, exultation and despair, and above all the *passion*. Surely that's the very stuff of poetry. This anthology began as part of the Langton Collection, an assembly of art and artefacts which illustrates the history of football, now part of the National Football Museum at Preston. As much as those rare paintings, sculptures, ceramics and curios and references to football in poetry illustrate the growth of the game from a simple kick-about pastime to the slick commercial enterprise it is today.

In 1987, when English football was at its lowest ebb, there was a London exhibition of the Langton Collection. After years of crowd violence, obscene and racial abuse both in the stands at home and hooliganism abroad, the exhibition was one man's attempt to show another side of the game.

In his catalogue Harry Langton wrote, "It is entirely wrong to suggest that the vast majority of football players and enthusiasts of all codes cannot appreciate finer things... This exhibition may also give encouragement to those who seek to restore English Football's tarnished reputation". Like some of those exhibits, a few of these poems may be rated as 'naive'. To quote again, "Nevertheless they are the honest art in football and seen together generate a powerful and colourful presence". I hope the same will be true of this book. Ann Langton

A Social Phenomenon Football has come to play an increasingly conspicuous role in social life in recent years. As the game's profile has been raised, attracting the interest of an ever wider cross-section of society across the world, so the phenomenon has also received greater attention from the arts. It is little surprise that many painters, sculptors, musicians and novelists have all sought inspiration in football, and found it with varying degrees of success. The dynamic nature of our sport, the beauty and fluidity of its movement, the passions it arouses and the breadth of its appeal to all ages and social classes, are no doubt but some of the reasons why it could not escape (and why should it?) the eye and the ear of the artist. Poetry, too, has drawn extensively upon the beautiful game and its environment. But here the phenomenon is less recent. The present collection reveals that verse has long been composed in honour of the game's practitioners, often with humour and invariably with affection, even at a time when it enjoyed a far less reputable social status than today. In the absence of factual documentation on football's evolution as a social force, these poetic compositions give us a fascinating and enriching insight into the role the game played in centuries well before the advent of Real Madrid, Juventus, Manchester United or the Champions League. Students of the game's history won't be surprised that it is in England, the cradle of the modern game, that there is a particularly rich vein of literature bearing direct and indirect reference to this most popular of all pastimes. Search as one may, there does not appear to be a comparable wealth of composition in other languages or cultures. The present collection of English football verse has been painstakingly assembled by Ann Langton in memory of her husband Harry, that most notable of collectors of football memorabilia. It is probably the most complete anthology of such work undertaken to date. To emphasise the international nature of the game, the collection has been supplemented by some offerings in French and German, generally of much more recent origin. Thus the current edition should include something to entertain most readers. We wish you every enjoyment from its pages.

Lennart Johansson. President of UEFA

Probably from the time that homo sapiens, having achieved balance on two legs, first put his toe to a stone and kicked it to a mate, who instinctively kicked it back.

Certainly it was long before such sport was recorded in language, written or sung. As time passed, early communities began introducing rules to their elementary play of kicking and throwing.

··

In some parts of the ancient world – China, Japan, Greece, the Roman Empire – football games developed as part of their ceremonial events, with the emphasis on style and artistry rather than brute strength.

··

Was football brought to Britain by the Roman military, as some believe? The earliest verses suggest, rather, that it took hold here as a pastime for children and country folk, a safety-valve for the energy and aggression of young males.

··

In one poem boys improvise a ball from a pig's bladder filled with dried peas. A couple of centuries later we read of bullock hide stuffed with hay: then, as now, the football hero was expected to be tough.

··

In town streets the play was even rougher. John Gay writes of the "furies of the football war", as clerks and apprentices charged through London's Covent Garden skittling pedestrians in their path.

··

Hero or villain, the football player had arrived as a force to be reckoned with in British national life.

QUEEN ELEANOR'S CONFESSION

anon

O don't you see two little boys
    Playing at the football?
O yonder is the Earl Marshall's son,
    And I like him best of all.

O don't you see yon other little boy
    Playing at the football?
O that one is King Henry's son,
    And I like him werst of all.

2

From a 13th century ballad
written to discredit Eleanor of
Aquitaine, Queen of Henry II,
suggesting in these verses
that one of the royal princes
was the son of the Earl Marshall.

LITTLE SIR HUGH OF LINCOLN

anon

Four and twenty bonny boys
Were playing at the ball,
And by it came sweet Sir Hugh,
And he played o'er them a'.

He kicked the ball with his right foot,
And catch'd it on his knee,
And through the Jew's window
He gard the bonny ball flee.

He's doen him to the Jew's castell,
And walked it round about;
And there he saw the Jew's daughter
At the window looking out.

"Throw down the ba', ye Jew's daughter
 Throw down the ba' to me.'
'Never a bit,' says the Jew's daughter,
'Till up to me come ye."

RUBAIYAT OF OMAR KHAYYAM

Edward Fitzgerald (1809 - 1893)

The ball no Question makes of Ayes and Noes,
But Right or Left as strikes the Player goes;
And he that toss'd Thee down into the Field,
He knows about it all – He knows – HE knows!

3

From an old English ballad dating
from the 13th century persecution
of the Jews of Lincoln. A charming
description of football play
prefaces a farago of anti-Semitism.

From Fitzgerald's 1859
translation of Omar Khayyam's
collection of quatrains (this is
no.50), discovered in a Persian
manuscript in the Bodleian
Library, Oxford. Khyayyam was
an eleventh century astronomer,
philosopher and poet.

BriSsit

banis,

Crui

u.

anon (16th century) THE BEWTEIS OF THE FUTE-BALL

awnis and broker tryf, discorde and waistie wanis eild syn halt withal Thir are the bewteis of the fute-ball

WINTER GAMES

Alexander Barclay (c.1475 - 1552)

Eche time and season hath his delite and joyes
Loke at the stretes, beholde the little boyes,
Howe in fruite season for joy they sing and hop,
In Lent is each one full busy with his top,
And nowe in winter for all the greevous colde,
All rent and ragged a man may them beholde,
They have great pleasour supposing well to dine,
When men get busied in killing of fat swine
They get the bladder, and blowe it great and thin
With many beanes and peason put within;
It ratleth, soundeth and shineth clere and fayre,
While it is throwen and caste up in the ayre.
Eche one contendeth and hath a great delite
With foote and with hande the bladder for to smite.
If it fall to grounde, they lift it up agayne
This wise to labour they count it for no payne.
Running and leaping they drive away the colde.
The sturdie plowmen lustie, strong and bolde
Ouercometh the winter with driving the foote ball,
Forgetting labour and many a grievous fall.

6

FROM   THE ILIAD OF HOMER

translation of George Chapman (1608)

This said, in poor Pisander's breast he fixt his weakful dart,
Who upward spread th' oppressed earth. His brother crouched for dread.
And as his lay, the angry king cut off his arms and head
And let him like a football lie for everie man spurne
Then to th'extremest heate of fight he did his valour turne
And led a multitude of Greeks...

ON A WELSH
TOMBSTONE

anon

Who ever hear on a Sunday
Will practis at the Ball
It may be before Monday
The Devil will Have you all.

Village 'ball fields' were often
adjacent to churches and
football was traditionally a
pastime for Sundays and
holy-days. The fact that
churchyards also sometimes
did service as pitches did
not help to make the game
popular with the clergy.

A bloodthirsty account of
the vengeance of Agamenon
refusing mercy to two young
brothers taken captive in
the Trojan Wars.

(overleaf)"Il calcio" at Padova. Engraving by Petro Bertelli circa 1595

THE ART OF WALKING THE STREETS OF LONDON

John Gay (1685 - 1732)

Where Covent Garden's famous temple stands.
That boasts the work of Jones' immortal hands;
Columns with plain magnificence appear,
And graceful porches lead along the square
Here oft' my course I bend, when lo! From far
I spy the furies of the foot-ball war:
The 'prentice quits his shop, to join the crew,
Increasing crowds the flying game pursue.
Thus, as you roll the ball o'er snowy ground,
The gathering globe augments with ev'ry round.
But whither shall I run? The throng draws nigh,
The ball now skims the street, now soars on high:
The dext'rous glazier strong returns the bound.
And ginging sashes on the pent-house sound.

From "Trivia", a poem of London life, describing a scene
in Covent Garden in 1716. Such boisterous games were a
danger to both neighbouring windows and passers-by.
A French visitor to London in 1728, M. Cesar de Saussure,
described a similar scene: "You sometimes see a score of
rascals in the streets kicking at a ball, and they will break
panes of glass and smash the windows of coaches, and
also knock you down...and when they knocked you down
they roared with laughter."

THE BALLAD OF JACK VOAN

anon

But wor'st foot bo' – ah wor indeed
Jack Voan hed hailed it down.
He pitched it reet owr't capstan heed,
An' then he went thro't town,
Sat striddle ways upon a plank,
They carried on their shoulders,
When't downy gyate gave brass or drink,
And uppy-gyates gave nowder.

THE SHROVETIDE SONG

anon

There's a town still plays this glorious game,
Tho' tis but a little spot.
And year by year the games still played,
From a field that is called Shawcroft,
Where friend meets friend in friendly strife,
The leather for to gain,
And they play the game right manfully,
In snow, sunshine or rain.

For loyal the game shall ever be,
No matter when or where,
And to treat the game as ought but free,
Is more than the boldest dare.
Thro' the ups and downs of its chequered life,
May the ball still ever roll,
Until by fair and gallant strife
We reach the treasured goal.

It's a good game
Deny it who can
That tries the pluck of
An Englishman

The

drunk k

tball

aughing-stock of Time

Tennyson THE PRINCESS

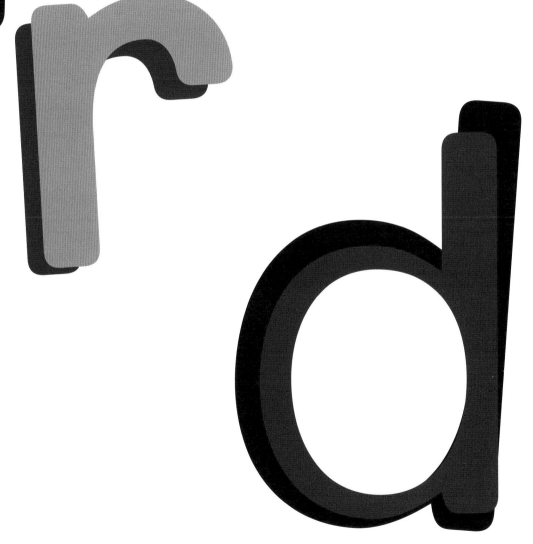

FROM   THE CHESTNUT TREE

Royall Tyler (1757 - 1826)*

And now up on the beaten soil,
    See, there the boisterous youngsters
    come;
Lads of the village, sons of toil
    Whose weekly drudgery is done.

With shout and rout the roistering throng
    Enjoy the hour of parting day,
And haul and drive their mates along
    To join the rude athletic play.

Some join the football's noisy war
    Or the sly wrestler's art they try,
Run, leap or pitch the massy bar
    Or send the bounding ball on high.

All hallowed be your manly sport,
    On you your Country's hopes abide:
In peace, the Union's sure support,
    In war, the nation's strength and pride.

14

FROM   THE EXCURSION

William Wordsworth (1770 - 1850)

And so, not wholly hidden from men's sight.
In him the spirit of a hero walked
Our unpretending valley, – How the quoit
Whizzed from the Stripling's arm! If touched by him.
The inglorious football mounted to the pitch
Of the lark's flight, – or shaped a rainbow curve,
Aloft, in prospect of the shouting field.

*An American writer remembered chiefly as
 a playwright.

FROM   A MATCH AT FOOT-BALL

Matthew Concanen (1701 - 1749)

While the bold youths arrang'd on either hand,
Around the field in decent order stand,
Among the throng lame Hobbinol appear'd
And waved his cap in order to be heard.
The green stood silent as the midnight-shade,
All tongues but his were still, when thus he said.
"Ye champions of fair Lusk, and ye of Soards,
View well this ball, the present of your Lords.
To outward view, three folds of bullock-hide,
With leathern thongs fast bound on ev'ry side:
A mass of finest hay conceal'd from sight,
Conspire at once to make it firm and light.
At this you'll all contend, this bravely strive,
Alternate thro' the adverse goal to drive,
Two gates of Sally, bound the spacious green
Here one, and one of yonder side is seen,
Guard that, ye men of Soards, ye others this,
Fame waits the careful, scandal the remiss.
He said, and high in air he flung the ball;
The champions crowd, and anxious wait its fall.

This long poem in three cantos, was printed in 1720
as a parody of Alexander Pope. In recounting the
story of a six-a-side match between two Baronies
in the Counties of Dublin, it gives what must be the
first running commentary of the game, with detailed
descriptions in which many elements of the modern
game can be recognised.

(overleaf) Postcard by Tom Browne, early 20th century

ON THE LIFTING OF THE BANNER OF THE HOUSE OF BUCCLEUCH, AT A GREAT FOOT-BALL MATCH ON CARTERHAUGH.

Sir Walter Scott (1771 - 1832)

From the brown crest of Newark its summons extending,
    Our signal is waving in smoke and in flame;
And each forester blithe, from his mountain descending,
    Bounds light o'er the heather to join in the game.

CHORUS

Then up with the Banner, let forest winds fan her,
    She has blazed over Ettrick eight ages and more;
In sport we'll attend her, in battle defend her,
    With heart and with hand, like our fathers before.

When the Southern invader spread waste and disorder,
    At the glance of her crescents he paused and withdrew,
For around them were marshall'd the pride of the Border,
    The Flowers of the Forest, the Bands of Buccleuch.

CHORUS

A Stripling's weak hand to our revel has borne her,
    No mail-glove has grasp'd her, no spearman surround;
But ere a bold foeman should scathe or should scorn her,
    A thousand true hearts would be cold on the ground.

CHORUS

We forget each contention of civil dissension,
　　And hail, like our brethren, Home, Douglas, and Car:
And Elliot and Pringle in pastime shall mingle,
　　As welcome in peace as their fathers in war,

CHORUS

Then strip, lads, and to it, though sharp be the weather,
　　And if, by mischance, you should happen to fall,
There are worse things in life than a tumble on heather,
　　And life is itself but a game at foot-ball.

CHORUS

And when it is over, we'll drink a blithe measure
　　To each Laird and each Lady that witness'd our fun,
And to every blithe heart that took part in our pleasure,
　　To the lads that have lost and the lads that have won,

CHORUS

May the Forest still flourish, both Borough and Landward,
　　From the hall of the Peer to the Herd's ingle-nook;
And huzza! My brave hearts, for Buccleuch and his standard,
　　For the King and the Country, the Clan, and the Duke!

CHORUS

Note: Scott, who has been described as "almost fanatical in his keenness for football", and at the time was Sheriff of the Forest of Ettrick, matched his team against one selected by the Earl of Home. The parties which assembled from the glens at Carterhaugh made a splendid sight with banners flying and pipes playing. Football was considered a better way of settling clan rivalries than acts of war.

A GAME OF BLOODY NOSES

"AS MUCH A BATTLE AS A SPORT"

+++++++++++++

is a fair description

of football games
in the 17th and 18th
centuries.

+++++++++++++

+++++++++++++

With violent scrummaging for the ball, running with it and throwing it, mass or mob football games ranged over town, country and stream.

Minor injuries were common, broken limbs not unusual, and a good soaking in the river to be expected.

Church holidays – Shrove Tuesday and Ash Wednesday especially – became traditional dates for a local derby.

Sometimes teams were composed of different sections of the community, such as the colliers and the sailors at Workington. Sometimes any able-bodied citizen was welcome to join in, and literally hundreds did.

"The noble duke, he gave a ball". Local lords were looked to for the provision of a fine ball, often matching their servants against those of neighbouring aristocrats. In Scotland, clan lined up against clan. Sir Walter Scott thought it a better way of settling rivalries than battles.

Traditional mass football games still survive in some parts of the UK. Distinctive, specially crafted – even handpainted – balls are used at places like Kirkwall (Orkney), Ashbourne (Derbyshire), and Workington (Cumbria).

Naturally, after-match analysis led to tales of heroic struggles to pass down to posterity. And naturally some took the form of ballads and songs. Read on.

- -
- -

FOOTBALL AT WORKINGTON

Gymnasticus (1824)

Behold the rival candidates for fame
Bent to engage in this adventurous game,
The foot-ball, at the word each scruple's quelled
And every thought of danger is dispell'd;
With gloomy courage, and affected glee,
The rivals meet – to brave their destiny –
Scowling defiance on th' opposing band:
These plough the stormy sea,
    and those the stubborn land.
Each party, ere the combat is begun
Looks on the vict'ry as already won,
And eyes the adverse force, with desperate spleen,
Such as young hearts will foster – brief and keen:
These view the landmen routed and dismay'd,
Those – Neptune's laurels with'ring in the shade.

Long ere the fierce contention had begun
Suspense increas'd, as dropped the setting sun;
And hordes poured in, be-garbed in rude attire,
Of coursest stuff prepar'd to meet the mire.
Oppos'd to this grim visag'd, earth-bred band
Stood the raw sailors, bolder in command
Than execution; yet their light limbs stood
The brunt of action, though with loss of blood.

The annual Shrove Tuesday match at Workington was
a wild contest between the Colliers (The Uppies) and
the Sailors (The Downies). Thousands watched and
hundreds joined in, with the action as much in the river
Derwent as on dry land.

The moment comes, and riot reigning now,
A keen solicitude mark'd ev'ry brow;
With solemn air, was thrown the bounding ball
And ev'ry eye was bent upon its fall.
The crush of strength each vig'rous rival spurn'd,
And ev'ry breast for nervous combat burned;
Each vein wax'd warm with renovated life,
Each sturdy youth was panting for the strife,
And sought the thickest fight with eager haste,
His heart, his arm, with hope of conquest brac'd.
The sons of ocean, long to hardship train'd
Against unequal numbers well maintain'd
The desperate conflict with the rustic crew –
Resolv'd to do "whatever men could do".
"By land, by water" boldly they engage
And roll in Derwent waters, but their rage
Not even Derwent's waters can assuage:
While on the banks the contest is renew'd
And tattered vestments on the ground are strew'd.

Now tailors smile, and thrifty housewives stare
Upon the widespread devastation there,
The crest-fall'n tars o'erwhelmed with grief and rage,
No longer can th' unequal warfare wage:
But scowling quit the field with tardy pace,
And with despair impress'd on ev'ry face
(The haggard fruits of many years' defeat),
While shouts of victory follow their retreat.

ASHBOURNE FOOTBALL

anon

If they get to the Park, the Upwards men shout,
And think all the Downwards men put to the rout,
But right about face they soon have to learn,
And the Downwards men shout and huzza in their turn.
Then into Shaw Croft, where the bold and the brave
Get a ducking in trying the foot-ball to save;
For 'tis well known they fear not a watery grave,
In defence of the football at Ashbourne.

Ashbourne, in Derbyshire, is one of the homes of a
Shrovetide game which rampaged though the streets
of the town and in the river Dove. This is from a long
ballard sung in 1821 by the comedian John Fawscett.

THE BLACKBURN ROVERS

anon

All hail, ye gallant Rover lads!
Etonians thought you were but cads!
They've found at football game their dads
    By meeting Blackburn Rovers.

CHORUS

So here's success to all the team,
Who carry the palm, who are the cream
Of footballing, and raise the steam
    To always win for the Rovers.

Who never to opponents yield
Their hard-earned laurels on the field,
For Sheffield "blades" although true steeled,
    Were fain to bend to the Rovers.

CHORUS

The English Cup, by brilliant play,
From Cockney land they bought away;
Let's hope in Blackburn it will stay
    To cheer the Blackburn Rovers.

CHORUS

Part of the poem published in leaflet form and distributed
before Blackburn met the Old Etonians, a London club, at
the Oval in the 1882 F.A. Cup final. Unhappily Blackburn
lost, a thrilling match ended in Old Etonians 1, Blacburn
Rovers 0.

(overleaf) Football in the streets of London. Etching by H. Heath, circa 1820

Now from the castle came the ball,
Out from the porch it flew, man,
Cheered the heart of every soul,
Each to his courage drew, man;
In Bailiffgate they kicked her fast,
And Narrowgate stood the hard blast,
The folk in Pottergate were fast.
The crowd like horse did smash, man.

ALNWICK FOOTBALL SONG

anon

Come listen to me, Sandy lad,
And I will tell you news, man,
What the lads of Alnwick had
To keep their feet in use, man,
The noble Duke he gave a ball
Oh let his name resound by all,
Both young and old, both great and small,
Sing o're his praise withal, man.
Sing o're his praise withal.

The ball then to the market flew,
The crowd they followed fast, man,
The kicks it made her black and blue,
Her very ribs were smashed, man;
They kicked her then up Bondgate street,
Just like a flock of highland sheep,
Some skinned their shins, some lamed their feet,
They ran so swift and fleet, man.

They kicked it then around the town,
Just like a butterfly, man,
For every skelp was like a drum,
It really was a spree, man;
Each ran at her to get a bat,
Another's trip would gar him stot,
Then down he'd come like any snot,
And tumbled like a block, man.

Each trade was active in its part,
The blacksmiths and the nailers,
Both millwrights and joiner lads,
The cobblers and the tailors;
The blacksmiths they did run with glee,
The nailers followed up the spree,
The cobbler says, 'It is for me,
For cunning and for sly, man'.

The slater and the ostler lads,
Look to be very keen, man,
The mason and the tailor lads
Were plodding to the e'en, man;
The ball then says, 'I'll have a drink,
Because the cobbler gave the wink';
The tailor cries, 'O Lord I'll sink,
My very heart plays clink, man'.

The mason he came creeping out,
Just like a half-drowned cat, man,
The water made him blubber up,
Just like a water rat, man;
'O Lord' he cried, 'I've had bad luck,
For in water like a duck,
I oft went down by ay came up,
And now I've got ashore, man.'

Tom has got home into the town,
Let's give him a huzza, man,
And drink a pint of good stout brown,
On the strength of the foot ball, man;
Here is a health unto his grace,
Landlords and Tenants of this place,
And every honest sonsy face,
Next year shall kick the ball, man.

At Alnwick ball some tore their coat,
And others peeled their shins, man,
Some shoes was torn off their feet,
And some had patched skins, man;
Some strained their arms and others legs,
Some on the ground got filthy pegs,
Were just a havoc like Mons Meg,
The ball went with such force, man.

Up Barney-side the ball took flight,
Tom ran just like a hare, man,
The dirt flew from his heels that night,
A full half mile and mair, man;
The gardeners of him got a sight,
Which put them all to running flight,
But Tommy bade them all good night,
He was so quick at flight, man.

I SAY-

WIZARD
TACKLE

NOT ALL GAMES WERE
UNREGULATED. BY THE
EARLY 1800's THE PUBLIC
SCHOOLS HAD DISCOVERED
FOOTBALL AS AN
EXCELLENT CHANNEL FOR
YOUTHFUL ENERGIES.

Problems arose because each school had its own
rules, varying according to tradition. This
brought confusion when the young gentlemen
played together at university.

At Cambridge in 1848 a group of men from Eton,
Harrow, Winchester, Rugby and Shrewsbury voted for
a set of common rules which were to be applied to
all games at the university.

Meantime football clubs were springing up in towns
all over the country. The arrival of the rubber
bladder was a key influence in the game.

In 1863 representatives of the leading clubs met at
the Freemasons' Tavern in Great Queen Street, London
to form the Football Association. So the term
'soccer' was born. The Cambridge rules formed the
basis of their discussions.

From this time charging, holding, tripping and
hacking were banned and the size of the pitch and
the ball regulated. Later nails, spikes and plated
boots were forbidden.

Not everyone agreed with the changes. Some thought
the game was getting soft.

But as the decades of the Victorian era passed the
principles of fair play, 'sleight of foot', and
brain rather than brawn prevailed. The game
developed into a more skilful display that was
attractive to watch.

And football was perceived as character forming,
making "men who can face good fortune or ill" as
one poem puts it.

THE GAME'S THE THING

anon

Short was the shout amid the rout;
The 'touchdown' soon may be
Annul'd in whole by the first "goal"
So off again the ball does roll,
Kicked from the goal line "free".
But soon again 'tis hurled back
With fist and hand, with kick and whack.

Kick at the ball or not at all. No pushing with the hand.
Tripping, holding, quar'ling, scolding
(Two umpires council holding
The play close watching stand);
No nails or spikes or plated boot,
The game is won by sleight of foot.

Strike if you list with hand or fist
The ball, but not the man!
No player hold, however bold,
But with your shoulder you are told,
Divert him if you can;
Lift or carry, lead they to ill –
Football's the game and won by skill.

Verses on a match between Queen's Park, Glasgow, and Hamilton Gymnasium, 1869.
The title is taken from the motto of Queen's Park Club – 'Ludas Causa Ludendi'.
Elements of Rugby and Soccer were still combined in games at this time. The men of
Queen's Park Club, founded 1867, preferred the 'dribbling' to the "handling" game
and followed the 1863 rules of the London Football Association. The Scottish Football
Association was not formed until 1873.

"Warm Work" by W J Hodgson, in private collection

PLAY UP!

E W Howson

Bother the ball, it goes so dead!
    Play up, you fellows, play up!
Rolling around like a lump of lead,
    Play up, you fellows, play up!
Who could play I should like to know
With half a ton at the end of his toe.★

CHORUS

Play up, you fellows, play up!
Who cares a jot, if a base be got,
Whether the game be killing or not
Play up, you fellows, play up!

No good trying, I can't go on!
    Play up, you fellows, play up!
Every morsel of wind is gone!
    Play up, you fellows, play up!
O for the ring of the welcome chime
Up on the Hill at the stroke of time!

CHORUS

Just the ankle I hurt before!
    Play up, you fellows, play up!
It always comes where the place is sore
    Play up, you fellows, play up!
And, sure as fate, if I charge it back
I lose the ball and I find a hack.

CHORUS

But better a toilsome game, say I
    Play up, you fellows, play up!
Than moon about in a coat and tie
    Play up, you fellows, play up!
And nothing will drive the dumps away
Like Harrow footer on Harrow clay!

CHORUS

34

From Harrow School Songs.
Part II 1885-1901.

★(overleaf) the Harrow
ball is considerably
larger than others

E W Howson

"Raining in torrents again," they say;
  The field is a slippery, miry marsh;
  But duty is duty, though sometimes harsh;
  And "footer" is "footer", whatever the day!

CHORUS

Yet the time may come as the days go by
When your heart will thrill
At the thought of the hill
And the slippery fields and the raining sky.

SING HEY FOR FOOTBALL!

anon

When the sun is hot and the sky is blue,
When golden September smiles fair on you,
And the team gather up, old hands and new –
Sing hey! Sing ho! for football.

When the fog rolls in and the sky is grey,
When the gloom steals down ere the close of day,
And you're only warm when the ball's your way –
Sing hey! Sing ho! for football.

When a cup-tie comes and the play is keen,
When there's just a hint of wigs on the green,
But right to the finish the game is clean –
Sing hey! Sing ho! for football.

The rough and tumble, the dash and the skill,
The single aim, and the curbing of will,
Make men who can face good fortune and ill –
Sing hey! Sing ho! for football.

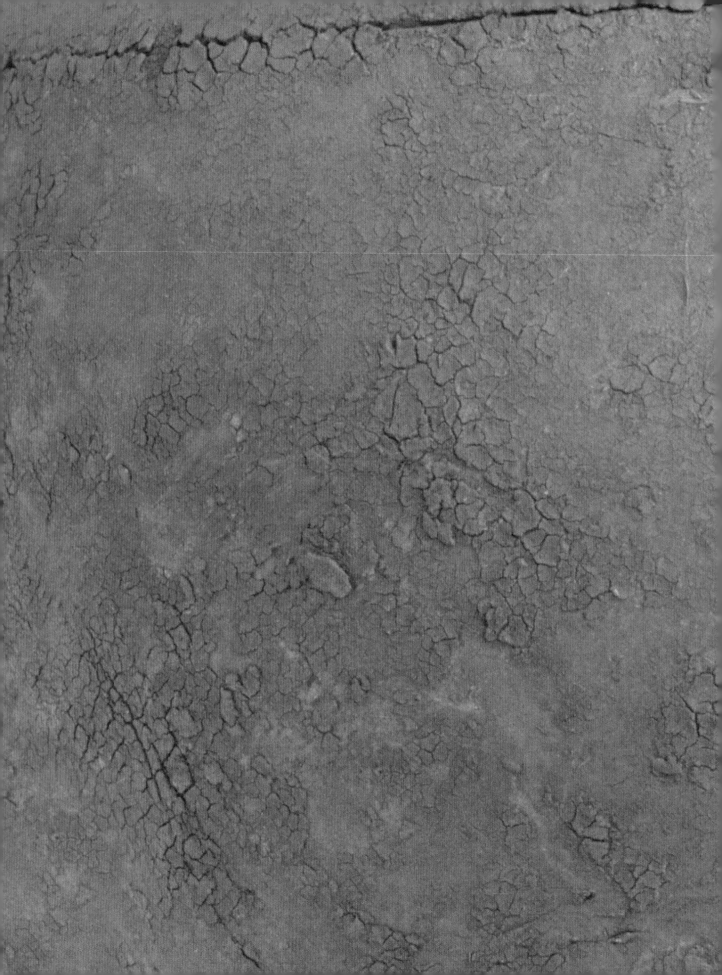

Having been instilled with the principles of fair play, courage and manliness, in 1914 the young men of Britain were called to display these qualities not on the sports field but on the battlefield.

And other elements were added: patriotism and the glory of sacrifice. Better to die for your country than earn honour by scoring goals. J D Rawnsley's "Appeal to the Football Player" makes chilling reading today.

As the appalling casualties mounted, virtually wiping out a generation of young men, the mood changed. Disenchanted poets who had enlisted and experienced the full horror of the war expressed its futility.

Wilfred Owen's "Disabled" tells of a boy footballer left limbless after he had lied about his age to join up. From his wheelchair he reflects on his folly.

And footballs, too, feature in war stories. A spontaneous 'friendly' with German troops took place in no-man's-land one Christmas Day. Afterwards both sides returned to their trenches and to fighting each other.

Some units kicked a ball ahead as they went 'over the top'. And generally footballs at the front must have been useful for the morale of the men.

After the war football became recognised as part of the English heritage, together with such images as John Bull, St George and a cup of tea.

TO **THE FOOTBALL PLAYER**

H D Rawnsley (1851 - 1920)

AN APPEAL

Play up the game! not yours a football goal,
Not with a leathern ball for pay you fight,
Your goal is freedom; champion of the right
You play to keep the British Empire whole,
Wherefore with body under full control,
Nerves strong as iron, sinews braced and tight,
You join the game with all the world in sight,
And losing life at least you win your soul.

Player of football! clear above the shame
Of thundering plaudits from a circling wall
Thunder of guns and cries of wounded come,
Your country bids you play a nobler game,
Forth to the front! tho' death the "time" may call,
Bright angel hosts shall cheer the victor home.

A ball at the battlefield. Calen Woodville print of World War 1 action –
an actual bayonet charge where the British infantry kicked footballs ahead of them

BREAKFAST

Wilfred Gibson (1878 - 1962)

We ate our breakfast lying on our backs
Because the shells were screaming overhead.
I bet a rasher to a loaf of bread
That Hull United would beat Halifax
When Jimmy Stainthorpe played full-back instead
Of Billy Bradford. Ginger raised his head
And cursed, and took the bet, and dropt back dead.
We ate our breakfast lying on our backs
Because the shells were screaming overhead.

FROM DISABLED

Wilfred Owen (1893 - 1918)

He sat in a wheeled chair, waiting for dark,
And shivered in his ghastly suit of grey,
Legless, sewn short at elbow. Through the park
Voices of boys rang saddening like a hymn,
Voices of play and pleasure after day,
Till gathering sleep had mothered them from him.

About this time Town used to swing so gay
When glow-lamps budded in the light blue trees,
And girl glanced lovelier as the air grew dim,
In the old times, before he threw away his knees.
Now he will never feel again how slim
Girl's waists are, or how warm their subtle hands.
All of them touch him like some queer disease.

There was an artist silly for his face,
For it was younger than his youth, last year.
Now, he is old; his back will never brace;
He's lost his colour very far from here,
Poured it down shell-holes till the veins ran dry,
And half his lifetime lapsed in the hot race
And leap of purple spurted from his thigh.

One time he liked a blood-smear down his leg,
After the matches, carried shoulder-high.
It was after football, when he'd drunk a peg,
Someone had said he'd look a god in kilts,
That's why; and maybe, too, to please his Meg,
Aye, that was it, to please the giddy jilts
He asked to join. He didn't have to beg;
Smiling they wrote his lie: aged nineteen years.

FROM A SHROPSHIRE LAD

A E Housman (1859 - 1936)

Twice a week the winter through
    Here I stood to keep the goal:
Football then was fighting sorrow
    For the young man's soul.

Now in Maytime to the wicket
    Out I march with bat and pad:
See the son of grief at cricket
    Trying to be glad.

Try I will; no harm in trying:
    Wonder 'tis how little mirth
Keeps the bones of man from lying
    On the bed of earth.

FROM   A SHROPSHIRE LAD

A E Housman (1859 - 1936)

'Is my team ploughing,
      That I was used to drive
And hear the harness jingle
      When I was man alive?'

Ay, the horses trample,
      The harness jingles now;
No change though you lie under
      The land you used to plough.

'Is football playing
      Along the river shore,
With lads to chase the leather,
      Now I stand up no more?'

Ay, the ball is flying,
      The lads play heart and soul;
The goal stands up, the keeper
      Stands up to keep the goal.

'Is my girl happy,
      That I thought hard to leave,
And has she tired of weeping
      As she lies down at eve?'

Ay, she lies down lightly,
      She lies not down to weep:
Your girl is well contented,
      Be still, my lad, and sleep.

'Is my friend hearty,
      Now I am thin and pine,
And has he found to sleep in
      A better bed than mine?'

Yes, lad, I lie easy,
      I lie as lads would choose;
I cheer a dead man's sweetheart,
      Never ask me whose.

Back in 1883 when Blackburn Olympic, a team
composed entirely of working men, won the
FA Cup, it was the end of an era in which the
amateurs-Wanderers, Oxford University, Old
Etonians and the like, ruled the game at club
level.

±±±

"The Toffs' Game" was fast becoming "The
People's Game". At the same time a crop of
new clubs in the North and Midlands held the
pragmatic view that money could buy success.

As a local spectacle attracting big gates
of fiercely partisan fans (fanatics), the game
became an 'experience' in which the crowd,
with its camaraderie and tribal chants, played
a major role. Poems in this section recall
times on the terraces with affection. All
discomforts were discounted in the exhilarating
atmosphere of the stadium.

By the second half of the century television
screens were bringing important matches into
living rooms. Controversial decisions were seen
in close up; cameras focused on ugly crowd
behaviour.

Now success for the clubs equalled vast
revenue from the TV providers. By the closing
years of the century transfer fees and the
wages of successful players soared to previously
unimaginable heights.

Many supporters wondered if the clubs had lost
the plot. Yet, however disillusioned they
were by the rule of mammon, enthusiasm for
football was undiminished. It remained a game
that could be enjoyed at all levels.

Nothing could change that.

±±±

FROM THE END OF THE 19th
century and through the
20th the growth of football,
now more correctly known
as 'soccer', accelerated
and spread throughout the
world.

THE CROWD

Robert Bridges (1844 - 1930)

FROM   TESTAMENT OF BEAUTY

Thus in our English sport, the spectacular games,
where tens of thousands flock throttling the entrance-gates
like sheep to th' pen, wherein they sit huddled to watch
the fortune o' the football, there is often here and there
mid the seething glomeration of that ugly embankment
of gazing faces, one that came to enjoy the sight
knowingly, and yet looketh little on the contest: to him
the crowd is the spectacle; its wrestle and agony
is more than the actors, and its contagion so thick
and irresistible, that ere he feel surprise
he too may find himself, yea philosophy and all,
carried away – as when a strong swimmer in the sea
who would regain the shore, is by the headlong surf
toss'd out of action, and like a drifted log roll'd up
breathless and unresisting on the roaring beach.

A shroud, a shroud for Spring-Heeled Jack,
The only honest referee,
A crowd to keep the devil back
And sing in tune Abide with Me.

DEATH OF THE REFEREE

Philip Oakes (1844 - 1930)

The pit unlocks its cage of doves
To tumble in the dirty air,
And far below the coffin drives
To meet the council and the mayor.

The barges drag through stiff canals,
Milky with clay and black with coal,
And as the varnished coffin falls
The mayor proclaims the grave no goal.

The colours of the local club
Flower to hide the yellow clay,
And all the foundry hammers throb
Their solace of the working day.

At home the silver trophies burn
About the mourning company,
And wishing she could be alone
The widow pours out cups of tea.

For Jack is dead, the man on springs,
Whose whistle trapped the wildest ball,
Whose portrait done in oils now hangs
For ever in the Civic Hall.

Burly with cataracts, the eyes,
Are blind at last to local fame
And friends who fail to recognise
A stranger in the golden frame.

But those who know their loss will make
The winter field his funeral,
And peel their caps to Spring-Heeled Jack
While brass bands play the March in Saul.

(overleaf) is an original
pamphlet for a 1895
women's match

Women's football teams were
organised as amateur sides
even before the First World
War. The Football Association
would not recognise ladies as
professional players, though
the fairer sex challenged
at many charity matches in
somewhat earnest spirit.
Armament workers at Preston's
Dick Kerr factory, one of the
better known teams, confronted
St Helen's Ladies on Boxing
Day 1920 watched by a
spectator crowd of 53,000.
It's perhaps unfortunate that
the event was not recorded
in verse.

49

THE FIRS

FOOTBAL

(NORTH

WILL BE

Saturday, 23r

UP

CROUCH END AT

NIGHTINGALE

LADIES'

MATCH

SOUTH)

YED ON

March, 1895,

HE

LETIC GROUND,

NE, HORNSEY.

OWDHAM FOOTBO'

Ammon Wrigley

It's run an' jump an' hop an' skip
An' sheawt hooray, an' hip, hip, hip,
It's singin' songs an' eytin tripe,
An' suppin' pints at single swipe,
An' brass for th' wife to buy a hat,
An' th' childer brass for this an' that,
An' beaucin' gaily up an' deawn,
Yo' connut find a merrier teawn,

When Owdham's won.

Aw lost mi brass, awm crabbed an' croat,
Aw lifted th' cat eawt wi' mi boot,
Awr ne'er as mad I' o mi life,
Cleautin' th' kids and' cursin' th' wife,
Awmn sure me brains han left mi yed,
Ther's nowt to do but goh toh bed,
At six o'clock o' th' seturdy neet,
They're o I' bed I' eawr street,

When Owdham's lost.

Goal!
    At that time he forgot
    The miseries of home, the creditors
    The going bald, the anodyne slavery

GOAL!

Alan Frost

Goal!
    At that moment he rose
    In vicarious triumph from the humdrum
    Of nothing life, of zero significance

Goal!
    At that moment he danced
    Wildly like a kid with the random carnival
    Of touchpaper deliquescence on the terrace

Goal!
    At that moment the simple bulge
    Of the white leather orb in a cage of netting
    Could erupt such ecstasy in his being

Goal!
    At that moment a dream lived
    Countless surreal desires were expatiated
    A hosanna phalanx of arms proclaimed

Goal!
    At that moment his heart jumped
    An evanescent climax freed him
    From the anchor of everyday thought

Goal!
    At that moment he scaled
    The apex of life
    For at that moment – he was happy

STANLEY MATTHEWS

Alan Ross

Not often *con brio*, but *andante, andante,*
Horseless, though jockey-like and jaunty,
Straddling the touchline, live margin
Not out of the game, nor quite in.
Made by him green and magnetic, stroller
Indifferent as a cat dissembling, rolling
A little as on deck, till the mouse, the ball,
Slides palely to him,
And shyly, almost with deprecatory cough, he is off.

Head of Perugino, with faint flare
Of the nostrils, as though Lipizzaner-like,
He sniffed at the air,
Finding the way open, uncluttered, draws
Defenders towards him, the ball a bait
They refuse like a poisoned chocolate,
Retreating, till he slows his gait
To a walk, inviting the tackle, inciting it.

At last, unrefusable, dangling the ball at the instep
He is charged – and stiffening so slowly
It is rarely perceptible, he executes with a squirm
Of the hips, a twist more suggestive than apparent,
That lazily disdainful move toreros term
A Veronica – it's enough.
Only emptiness following him, pursuing some scent
Of his own, he weaves in towards
Not away from, fresh tacklers,
Who, turning about to gain time, are by him
Harried, pursued, not pursuers.

Now gathers speed, nursing the ball as he cruises,
Eyes judging distance, noting the gaps, the spaces
Vital for colleagues to move to, slowing a trace
As from Vivaldi to Dibdin, pausing,
And leisurely, leisurely, swings
To the left upright his centre, on hips
His hands, observing the goalkeeper spring,
Heads rising vainly to the ball's curve
Just as it's plucked from them; and dispassionately
Back to his mark he trots, whistling through closed lips.

Trim as a yacht, with similar lightness
– of keel, of reaction to surface – with salt air
tanned, this incomparable player, in decline fair
to look at, nor in decline either,
improving like wine with age, has come far –
born to one, a barber, who boxed
not with such filial magnificence, but well.
'The greatest of all time,' *meraviglioso*, Matthews –
Stoke City, Blackpool and England.
Expressionless enchanter, weaving as on strings
Conceptual patterns to a private music, heard
Only by him, to whose slowly emerging theme
He rehearses steps, soloist in compulsions of a dream.

Detail from "Big Match" Edwin Scott early 1950's

FROM   ZIGGER ZAGGER

Peter Terson

At the match

HARRY: Come Saturday,
The whole town comes alive,
People are going one way,
From all the streets,
They are going the one way,
And meeting and joining,
And going on and meeting more and more
Till the trickle becomes a flood.
And men are so packed tight
That the cars have to nose their way through.
And you come to the stadium,
And it's humming,
A hum comes from the bowl.
And the people inside seem to be saying,
Come on in, come on in,
And you jostle at the turnstile,
And the turnstile clicks and clicks,
And you push nearer and nearer,
Through the dark gap,
Then you're in.
And the great stand of the City end,
It's like a hall,
A great hall,
And you go on,
Through the arch
And you see the pitch,
Green, new shaven and watered,
And the groundsman's made the white lines,
As straight as a ruler,

Scene Eighteen:

And the ash is pressed.
And you find your place amongst the fans,
The real fans,
The singers and chanters and rattle wavers,
And a sheet of tobacco smoke hangs over the crowd.
And the crowd whistles and hoots,
And the policemen circling the pitch
Look up and know they're in for a rough day of it,
And the stadium fills up,
The Open End first, then the City End,
Then the paddock, then the covered seated stand,
Then, last of all, the fat directors
With the Lord Mayor and cigars.
And the reporters are in their little glass box,
And the cameramen position themselves
By the goal,
And there's a looking down the tunnel,
Then a hush.
Then out they come.
The lads,
Like toy footballers on a green billiard table.
And the roar goes up...

CHORUS   (general roar; all sing)
City City, City City,
We'll support you evermore,
We'll support you evermore.
City City, City City,
We'll support you evermore,
We'll support you evermore.

Zigger Zagger was first performed by the
National Youth Theatre in 1967.

THE GAME

Danny Abse

Follow the crowds to where the turnstiles click.
The terraces fill. Hoompa, blares the brassy band.
Saturday afternoon has come to Ninian Park
And. Beyond the goalposts, in the Cannon Stand
Between black spaces, a hundred matches spark.

Waiting, we recall records, legendary scores:
Fred Keenor, Hardy, in a royal blue shirt.
The very names, sad as the old songs, open doors
Before our time where someone else was hurt.
Now, like an injured beast, the great crowd roars.

The coin is spun. Here all is simplified
And we are partisan who cheer the Good,
Hiss at passing Evil. Was Lucifer offside?
A wing falls down when cherubs howl for blood.
Demons have agents: the Referee is bribed.

The white ball smacks the crossbar. Satan rose
Higher than the others in the smoked brown gloom
To sink on grass in a ballet dancer's pose.
Again, it seems, we hear a familiar tune
Not quite identifiable. A distant whistle blows.

Memory of faded games, the discarded years;
Talk of Aston Villa, Orient and the Swans.
Half-time, the band played the same military airs
As when the Bluebirds once were champions.
Round touchlines, the same cripples in their chairs.

Mephistopheles had his joke. The honest team
Dribbles ineffectually, no one can be blamed.
Infernal backs tackle, inside forwards scheme,
And if they foul us need we be ashamed?
Heads up! Oh for a Ted Drake, a Dixie Dean.

'Saved' or else, discontents, we are transferred
long decades back, like Faust must pay that fee.
The Night is early. Great phantoms in us stir
As coloured jerseys hover, move diagonally
On the damp turf, and our eidetic visions blur.

God sign our souls! Because the obscure Staff
Of Hell rules this world, jugular fans guessed
The result half way through the second half
And those who know the score just seem depressed.
Small boys swarm the field for an autograph.

Silent the Stadium. The crowds have all filed out.
Only the pigeons beneath the roofs remain.
The clean programmes are trampled underfoot,
And natural the dark, appropriate the rain
Whilst, under lampposts, threatening newsboys shout.

Abroad, an alien, at home, an outlaw.

M.A. Shee ALASCO

THE OLD TEAM

Seamus Heaney

Dusk. Scope of air. A railed pavilion
Formal and blurring in the sepia
Of (always) summery Edwardian
Ulster. Which could be India
Or England. Or any old parade ground
Where a moustachioed tenantry togged out
To pose with folded arms, all musclebound
And staunch and forever up against it.

Moyola Park FC! Sons of Castledawson!
Stokers and scutchers! Grandfather McCann!
Team spirit, walled parkland, the linen mill
Have, in your absence, grown historical
As those lightly clapped, dull-thumping games of football
The steady coffins sail past at eye-level.

MARKINGS

Seamus Heaney

We've marked the pitch: four jackets for four goalposts,
That was all. The corners and the squares
Were there like longitude and latitude
Under the bumpy thistly ground, to be
Agreed about or disagreed about
When the time came. And then we picked the teams
And crossed the line our called names drew between us.

Youngsters shouting their heads off in a field
As the light died and they kept on playing
Because by then they were playing in their heads
Like a dream heaviness, and their own hard
Breathing in the dark and skids on grass
Sounded like effort in another world...
It was quick and constant, a game that never need
Be played out. Some limit had been passed,
There was fleetness, futherance, untiredness
In time that was extra, unforseen and free.

(overleaf) Wembley Cup Final 1951 by Henry Deykin.

Jackie Milburn has just scored for Newcastle against Blackpool.
Newcastle won 2-0, Milburn scoring both goals. (Henry Cotteril Deykin,
born Edgbaston 1905, exhibited Royal Academy and Provinces)

FOOTBALL AT SLACK

Ted Hughes (1930 - 1998)

Between plunging valleys, on a bareback of hill
Men in bunting colours
Bounced, and their blown ball bounced.

The blown ball jumped, and the merry-coloured men
Spouted like water to head it.
The ball blew away downwind –

The rubbery men bounced after it.
The ball jumped up and out and hung on the wind
Over a gulf of treetops.
Then they all shouted together, and the ball blew back.

Winds from fiery holes in heaven
Piled the hills darkening around them
To awe them. The glare light
Mixed its mad oils and threw glooms.
Then the rain lowered a steel press.

Hair plastered, they all just trod water
To puddle glitter. And their shouts bobbed up
Coming fine and thin, washed and happy

While the humped world sank foundering
And the valleys blued unthinkable
Under depth of Atlantic depression –

But the wingers leapt, they bicycled in air
And the goalie flew horizontal

And once again a golden holocaust
Lifted the cloud's edge, to watch them.

WORLD CUP

Alan Ross

It is, after all, a kind
Of music, an elaborating of themes
That swell and subside, which
In the converting of open spaces
Take on a clean edge.
A throw, a chip,
A flick, Wilson to Charlton,
To Moore, to Hunt, to Greaves –
The diagonals cross, green space is charmed.

A precise movement, balletic in ordained
Agility, with the players as if magnetised
Moving into places seemingly allotted them
– They seem from above to be pushed like counters
And only the fluffed pass, the momentary
Crudity disconcerting as a clerical oath,
Destroys the illusion. A goal restores it.

Arms raised like gladiators, they embrace.
Human emotions swamp them, childishly even
For such protagonists of perfection.
And involved in this mixture
Of the fallible and the dreamy,
The percussive and the lilting, they demonstrate
How art exists on many levels, spirit
And matter close-knit as strangling lianas.

HOW PROTESTANT ULSTER WON THE WORLD CUP

Andrew Waterman

We faced the whole menagerie, a mix
Of Papists, atheists, other heretics.
The Poles? Chopped. Dutch? Ditched. Cameroons?
No hope,
Them darkies couldn't knock snow off a rope.
We played as in the bygone days of yore –
It wasn't sweepers or a flat back four
Won King Billy glory at the Boyne,
But thranness, strike-rate, crunching skull and groin.
Brazil in the quarter-final tried all tricks,
Backheels, swerves, dummies, one-twos, bicycle-kicks;
They'd not last one late night in Newtownards.
The ref was sprouting red and yellow cards.
Bookings, was it? – wee Sam fetched him a skelp
With the Good Book, you should have heard him yelp.
'No artistry, technique, footballing ideals,'
Carped critics, 'No coach, bar that wreck on wheels!'
Aye, we've no truck with such idolatries,
Newfangled texts, quare diets, shrinks, spin-off fees.
Fired up on the Ulster Fries we love,
The only sponsor we need's Him Above.
The semis was Germany. See Fritz's running

Off the ball, us in pursuit! He's cunning;
Dives in the box, greetins and girnins, till
He'd conned a spot-kick, stroked it home: 1-0.
We upped our game. Now they weren't shamming dead.
Their goalie picked up, looked to throw – instead
Was hit by Billy going like a train
Clean through the net, we're back on terms again.
Penalty shoot-out. We'd trained using live
Rounds in the Mournes, no way Fritz could survive.
As the smoke cleared a staunch voice sounded from
The stand: 'Next time, we'll replay at the Somme!'
The media boys were cracking up, the Pope
Redd out the Vatican for a hank of rope.
Our team, in orange sashes, brave and broad,
Lined up to put the Spaniards to the sword.
The rest is history. Our names resound
From Strabane to Strangford, Erne to Rathlin Sound.
Them dancers pushed the ball round smooth as silk.

Big Willie John turns slower than the milk,
But he'd not give an inch. He dug a trench.
(There was some noise upon it from their bench).
See Jim's Jack Russell, Hughie's Kerry Blue,
They'd not be bluffing, took a limb or two.
We buried the Fenians; then the referee,
And lifted the World Cup in victory:
'Yousuns get back to your fancy hacienda –
What we have we hold, and no surrender!'

He raised it high again, swigged, jack-knifed, boked
The barman said, 'the eejit's went and choked.'
The great Ref in the Sky had blown Offside;
His fantasy exploded as he died.
Yet through Infernal smoke he made out more
Who'd got the worlds they'd once been asking for:
Midas deranged by gold he couldn't spend;
Stalin patrolling gulags without end;
Romeo cursed with Juliet at his throat;
Academics doomed to read the stuff they wrote.
For him, a rain-swept divot, and the thrum
Of bigoted sermonising, Lambeg drum;
Great gales stentorian with ancient malice;
Still dead-weight on his lap the poisoned chalice.

G. LINEKER

Alan Ross

A style suggested by a name,
A way of comportment, of playing –
In the merging of 'line' and 'glint'
Necessary elusiveness, hint
Of mother of pearl, 'nacreous',
As in the opening, knife-edged,
Of two halves of an oyster.

In the music of Satie there is
Similar opportunism, echoes
And chances taken up, exploited –
'Striker' and 'Lion', a 'cur'
Hanging around on the off-chance.
Something dabbled, as in a painting
By Seurat, linked dots
That on good days veer towards fable.

THE BEAUTIFUL GAME (PELE)

Andrew Waterman

This summer's drained of vivid promises,
A chill negation of what should have been:
Betrayed from which, I slump among what is,
Watch World Cup football flicker on my screen,
It too falls short, squanders in dreariness,
Unjust results, gifts thwarted, patternless.
Useless in memory glow Pele's sway
Dummying that goalie, ghost-glides of Tostao.
Yet like life too this game will never fail
Us quite, slips leaden days by alchemising
From battle to romance: that through-pass now,
A juggling run, the net shakes, and I'm rising
To beauty opened like a peacock's tail.

O FUTEBOL
a song dedicated to Pele (c.1989)

Chico Buarque
popular Brazilian singer,
song writer and novelist.

Hitting the net
With a dream of a goal
If only
I were Pele the King
Striking my songs
Home
A painter measuring exactly
To hang in a gallery, no
Brushstroke's more perfect
Than a goal shot
Crisp
As an arrow or a dry leaf.

WONDER BOY

Jeff Cloves

And so
Among the traded playground fagcards
He found his once and only heroes
And learned by heart
The minute biographies
Of wingers and centre forwards
With centre partings
Brilliantined hair
Blue chins
Knotted arms folded across
Striped jerseys
Clinging to manly chests
Bulbous eyes fixed on the lens
Of the brass and mahogany box
And the hunch-back
Black-draped photographer

And so the heroes of Wednesday Albion & Hotspur
Beamed their psychic messages
Across the years
To the child of the forties
Who dreamed
Not only of Stella Coxon
Who shared his pitchpine desk at school
But of Dixie Dean
And Alex James
Played every night at Wembley
Received the cup from the King
And was borne shoulder high
Round the ground
To the sound
Of brass bands and cheering crowds
And dreamed
He turned at last
To the sticky kiss of the patient Stella
Who stood on tiptoe
High upon the sleepy dreamtime terraces
At every game he played
To see her wonder boy come through
And score the winning goal always
Always
In the last
Minute
Of extra
Time

HOME SUPPORT

Ian McMillan

It is mid-July, 1997. It is hot.
Barnsley are in the PREMIER LEAGUE,
And in my head our season
Is laid out as simple as an Underground Map,
Or a child's drawing of the solar system.
Mid-July, a pre-season friendly
Against Doncaster. The start of something
And one my daughters is coming to Doncaster
On her own for the first time on the bus
To meet me to go to the match. As the bus
Rolls into the bus station I see her red shirt
Upstairs, and she waves, and my heart breaks.

For her, and me, and her red shirt with 21 TINKLER
On the back, and the bus driver who is a Middlesborough fan,
And the other people who tumble off the bus in their red shirts
With the season laid out in their heads simple and lovely
As a map of the solar system or a child's drawing
Of the Underground, and the Greek bus station toilet attendant
Who knows me and shouts PREMIER LEAGUE, but
Mostly it breaks for her, and me, and her red shirt.

Still, it's July. It's hot. We meet Chris and Duncan
And we try to go into a pub even though my daughter's
A bit young and a man in a suit says Sorry, Home Support Only.
And my heart breaks
For her, and me, and her red shirt, and the Home Support
Who cheer Doncaster and whose season is laid out simple
As a serving suggestion, or a child's drawing of a football team,
But mostly it breaks for her and me.

We get a taxi home, which seems extravagant, but I think
Of the Greek toilet attendant and I shout PREMIER LEAGUE
On our path as we walk into the house, father and daughter, red
Shirt, hot night, Home Support, season laid out in our heads
Simple and lovely as a football programme, simple and lovely
As a penalty kick, a well-taken corner.

75

THE PITCH

Matthew Sweeney

The goals are crooked on the snowy pitch
But errant shots won't score today,
Won't kindle a school-burning controversy.
And no-one sleeps on the centre circle
In an orange tent, refusing to leave,
Reminding the Head through a zipped door
That the lunches are execrable, the loos
Public, the everyday laws childish.
The muffled reporter (and one-time student)
Won't find a story here, not unless
She imagines well and wields a grudge
And she's much too ambitious for that.
A mouse lies stiff in the penalty area,
Smoke shadows the perimeter trees,
Footprints traverse the piebald surface
On the shortcut to the go-slow trains.

I'm an ordinary feller 6 days week
But Saturday turn into a football freak,
I'm schizofanatic, sad but it's true,
One half of me's red, and the other half's blue.

FOOTY POEM

Roger McGough

I can't make my mind up which team to support
Whether to lean to starboard or port
I'd be bisexual if I had time for sex,
Cos it's Goodison one week and Anfield the next.

But the worst time of all is Derby day
One half of me's at home and the other's away
So I get down there early all ready for battle
With me rainbow scarf and me two-tone rattle.

And I'm shouting for Lachford and I'm shouting for Hughes
'Come on de Pool' – 'Gerrin dere Blues'
'Give it ter Keegan' – 'Worra puddin'
'King of der Kop' – all of a sudden – Wop!

And after the match as I walk back alone
It's argue, argue all the way home.
Some nights when I'm drunk I've even let fly
An give meself a poke in the eye.

But in front of the fire watchin 'Match of the Day'
Tired but happy, I look at it this way:
Part of me's lost and part of me's won
I've had twice the heartache – but I've had twice the fun.

NOOLIGAN

Roger McGough

I'm a nooligan
Don't give a toss
In our class
I'm the boss
(well, one of them)

I'm a nooligan
Got a nard 'ead
Step out of line
And you're dead
(well, bleedin)

I'm a nooligan
I spray me name
All over town
Football's me game
(well, watchin)

I'm a nooligan
Violence is fun
Gonna be a nassassin
Or a hired gun
(well, a soldier)

Three cheers for Spurs!
They beat Stoke!
Glad I'm a football fan.
Glad I'm a bloke.

ROGER BEAR'S FOOTBALL POEMS

Wendy Cope

Who beat Liverpool
Then beat them again?
Tottenham Hotspur –
A bunch of real men.

Tottenham lost
And I am sad.
Sometimes it's difficult
Being a lad.

Spurs beat Newcastle,
Just like I reckoned
Spurs are brilliant
And now they are second.

Will they beat Everton?
We'll have to see
Please get a ticket
For Wendy and me.

KICK FOOTBALL

LIKE YOU KICK YOUR WIFE

Adrian Mitchell WORLD CUP SONG (for the Scottish team)

KICK THAT FOOTBALL

like you kick

YOUR MOTHER

KICK THAT FOOTBALL

like you kick your

CHILDREN

FOOTBALLS

NEVER . KICK BACK

GOAL

Gerard Benson

It's Dicky to Dirty
And Dirty back to Dicky...
He swerves past three men
(Oh, he's tricky)
And he lofts the ball
Into the middle,
A pin-point pass,
Which finds Diddle;
Diddle back-heels
(Very neat that, clever!)
and lays it in the path
of Trevor
our six million pound
striker (well 25 pee
if you want the truth)
and he
drives it, right-footed;
it strikes the bar
and rebounds into the path
of Pa
(Our oldest player)
but unluckily it hits
his walking stick....
He sits
Suddenly, and the ball
Trickles back to Trevor
Who shoots!! Unstoppable!!!
Did you ever!?!?
Their goalie palms
it away but straight
To Dozy (who's asleep)
But wait...!
Patch has got the ball
(he's half collie –
Recently signed from Rovers)
And, golly!
He's nose down, tail up –
He's running rings
Round a sheepish defence –
He brings
The leather to the educated feet
Of Gerard⋆ (You bet!)
Now one neat flick and it's
In the net!

⋆Note: Or, if you wish, put your own name as a late substitute.

82

THE FOOTBALL GHOSTS

Gerard Benson

At night, when the stadium is empty,
When the grass in the moonlight is silver-grey,
When the goals look like hungry fishing nets,
It is then the old ghosts play.

When all the crisp packets and fag-ends
And the drink cans have been swept up,
And the crowds have left, and the gates are locked,
They play for the Phantom Cup.

Thin clouds drift across the face of the moon,
The grass stirs, a preeping whistle sounds,
And silent invisible spectators
Throng the deserted stands.

And twenty-two ghosts in long-legged shorts
Dance the ball across the silvered grass,
A ball you can almost see, the old game –
Run, dribble and pass.

Pale shades and shadows, heroes of bygone days.
Under the gaze of the moon, sidestep and swerve,
And crowds silently cheer as the ball floats
Goalward in an unseen curve.

PLAYING WITH NUMBERS

Jeff Cloves

When I was a schoolboy
and sweet Saturday came
I stood upon the terraces
to watch the People's Game
each player was perfection
each classic shirt delight
each position had its number
from left-back to outside-right
the centre-forward was our flag
number 9 upon his back
the goalie in green jersey
the referee wore black
one - two - three - four
it's the game that we adore

But football now is opera
(the tickets cost the same)
every prima donna player
adds millions to his fame
numbers now don't mean a thing
inside forwards are passé
and centre-halves and wingers all
belong to yesterday
'cause the People's Game got stolen
in a money-making maul
now it's hard to find the People
in the Business of football
five - six - seven - eight
the game that we appreciate

It's on parks and fields and marshes
that you'll find the People's Game
played by boys and girls and young men
with no money to their name
their line-ups follow fashion
their shirt numbers are awry
– though there's no TV to track then
from the golden-vaulted SKY –
and the strikers and the sweepers
and the wing-backs all still play
the game I remember
and my dad played in his day
one - two - three - four - five - six - seven
eight - nine - ten - and the winger's eleven
football football one - two - three
the people's game for you and me
football football one - two - three
the people's game for everybody

AMERIKA

Sean O'Brien

The subtleties are wasted on the Yanks.
They like their football players built like tanks.
And find it hard to understand that skill
May well produce a scoreline of nil-nil.

A journalist in Minneapolis
Enquired. 'Hey, what kind of crap is this?'
The Majors' baseball strike had cancelled out
What all his summer columns were about.

And he'd been sent to watch Bulgaria's
Brilliant but nefarious
Stoichkov-Lechkov-Kostadinov team
Punch holes in half of football's so-called cream –

Although this fact had somehow passed him by.
It seemed to his uneducated eye
This game was kind of complicated, weird
And somehow even longer than he feared.

'This thing,' he said, 'has possibilities.
But let me tell you how it really is.
America means short attention span,
So let me run some changes past you, man.

'We want a wider goal, a bigger ball.
We want real bricks in the defensive wall.
We want the pitch divided into four
Plus fifteen time-outs making room for more.

'Commercials. That, my friend's what we call sport.'
Poor sod, one more imagination bought
And rented out to commerce as a site
Where money = nation = right.

It seemed from watching the Atlanta Games
Amercians alone possess their names;
That those who came to represent elsewhere
Might just as well not bother being there.

Of course this wasn't a deliberate act
But it revealed a national want of tact.
America exists to be the best:
And second's nowhere; second's for the rest.

But I remembered, while the strike was on,
How this friend's friend and I had one day gone
To watch a minor league game in the sticks –
A bunch of has-beens taking on the hicks.

That summer's end between two railroad yards
Were men whose lives were faded baseball cards,
Who wound it up and from their far-gone youth
Unleashed in dreams the balls that baffled Ruth.

Or hammered one past Nolan Ryan's ears –
The kind of thing a failure stands and cheers:
When all you are's a mortgage and a job
You'd like to kick the crap from Tyrus Cobb.

Or pass Ted Williams' average by a street.
This is your other life, the short and sweet:-
The afternoon when you're DiMaggio
And some girl wants to meet you, called Munroe...

All that was just a trick played by light,
But since then, if I have a sleepless night
I listen for the sound of far-off trains
Like those that carried teams across the plains –

To me they sound like poems in the air
By those who write their epics then and there:
An hour's enough for immortality,
And if they had to they'd still play for free.

85

(overleaf) "Shoot, Shoot..." Cartoon for the London "Evening Standard", 1970

"Shoot, shoot, what are you waiting for— a drama award?"

FOOTBALL! FOOTBALL! FOOTBALL!

Sean O'Brien

My sporting life (may I refer to me?)
Was never all it was supposed to be.
Mine was a case of talent unfulfilled.
I blame society, which blames my build.

From trap and pass and backheel in the yard
To deskbound middle age is something hard
For the Eusebio of '64
To grasp: you don't play football any more.

Your boots and kit are all gone into dust,
And your electric pace a shade of rust.
Whatever knocks the football fates inflict
On Shearer now, your chance of being picked.

If England reach the Mondiale in France
(Does Umbro really make that size of pants?)
Is smaller than the risk of being brained
By frozen urine falling from a plane.

And though you'll stop by any rainy park
To watch folks kick a ball until it's dark,
You don't expect Dalglish will seek you out
To ask you what the game is all about.

But more fool him, you secretly suspect:
You've seen the lot, from Crewe to Anderlecht,
From Gornik to Stranraer to River Plate,
The Cosmos and Montrose and Grampus Eight.

The Accies, Bochum, Galatasaray,
Finbogdottir, Dukla Prague (away),
Botafogo, Bury, Reggiana...
Football! Football! Football! Work? Mañana.

Sponsored by IKEA and by Andrex
Butch in sacks or mincing on in Spandex,
The great, the mediocre, the pathetic,
Real Madrid and Raggy-Arse Athletic –

Twelve quid a week or fifty grand an hour,
The game retains the undiminished power
To stop the clock, accelerate the blood
And sort the decent geezer from the crud.

From 5-3-2 to Kaiser Franz libero
Is there a team formation you don't know?
Experience! There is no substitute
When working out why Andy Cole can't shoot.

The fields of dream and nightmare where the great
Line up beside the donkeys to debate
Who gets the league, the cup, the bird, the chop
And whether Coventry deserve the drop.

Are graveyards of a century's desire
To keep the youth that sets the world on fire –
Pele's '58, Diego's '86,
And Puskas hushing Wembley with his tricks...

And back, and back, to James and Meredith
And all the tricky Welsh who took the pith,
Until West Auckland marmalize Juventus –
World on world through which the game has sent us.

Until at last we stand in some back lane.
You're Cantona but I'll be Best again.
Who gives a toss what any of it means
While there are Platinis and Dixie Deans?

There life is always Saturday, from three
Till Sports Report, as it's supposed to be,
The terrace in its shroud of freezing breath,
Hot leg, crap ref, a soft goal at the death.

Fags and Bovril, bus home, bacon sandwich –
Paradise in anybody's language
Is listening for the fate of Stenhousmuir
(Robbed by Brechin 27-4).

A

FUNNY
OLD

GAME

"Lucky for some; for some, bad medicine". Forecasting the result of any match is a chancy business. Players injured, players off-form, penalties, and so on, all blamed on luck, fate, ju-ju, and even the hand of God.

So we have Gazza writing ruefully from his hospital bed, and John Toshack thanking a freak storm for his place in an historic game.

/ /

As for the ball, that is seen as a dispassionate object, a random instrument of fate. It is not its job to take sides.
And unfairly, because it is kicked, it is frequently a symbol of something despised.

/ /

On the other hand the game itself is held up by a 1st century Chinese philosopher as a model for how we should live our lives.

/ /

Equally stern is the reminder that 'playing the game' in both senses of the phrase is more important than winning.

/ /

And to complete the range of poems we can offer one that is somewhat surreal, as Golo, the Gloomy Goalkeeper, falls in love with the grass on the pitch. It's a romance with a happy ending.

/ /

JUST ME

Paul Gascoigne

I'm a professional footballer
lying in a hospital bed
thinking of all those nasty things
all going through my head.

I know I should not be lying here
it's because of Wembley
thinking of that stupid tackle
instead of all that glee.

Now when I do get out of here
I'll be working on this knee
getting fit left, right and centre
just thinking of Italy.

Now what is on my mind right now
no one will ever know
but when I'm given my big, big chance
it will be a one man show.

Now Mel and Len* both work for me
both working day and night
one's an accountant
one's a lawyer
making sure I'm alright.

Now please don't worry about a thing
I know I'm getting thinner
but at the back of my mind
there'll only be one winner.

92

*Mel Stein, his accountant
and Len Lazarus, his lawyer.

Gazza faxed this from Italy in 1993 for a book
in aid of the Malcolm Sargeant Cancer Fund.
He was one of only two people (Barbara Cartland
was the other), to submit their own work.

UNTITLED

Fiona Pitt-Kethley

Gazza, though you're sheer poetry on the field,
Your athlete's hands were never framed to wield
A pen. Your brain is in your legs and cannot rise
Above those well-built, gladiatorial thighs,

Your surname shows your forbears came from France.
The Gascons led the rest a merry dance –
They were the butt of Medieval jokes –
And starred in such as idiots, gluttons, soaks,

There have been some illustrious Gascoignes, though.
George was the best – four hundred years or so
Before you penned your lines, he filled his days
By writing poems, translations, satires, plays.

An epic, too. Now, there's a frightful thought...
If you must write, Paul, please do keep it short.

93

Responses in the 'Independent'
August 29, 1993.

SONNET: AWAY GAMES

Gavin Ewart

Some agro from a Roumanian referee
The ball bouncing unevenly. Skidding on the mud.
An acting-injured jersey-pulling opposition.
The crowd with klaxons, noise to blow the mind.
One unearned penalty. That, you might say, was it.
If it's against you, then it's all against you,
the gods of football haven't heard of justice;
like poetry, the word 'fair' won't translate.

For us the world is one huge object found,
random with art and wars and income tax,
the very lack of pattern is a pattern;
as it swivels through space, an awkward
high ball in the air, it's lucky or unlucky.
Lucky for some; for some, bad medicine.

"The Game of the Year"
by Ithell Colquhoun, 1953

YOU NEVER KNOW

John Toshack

We battled hard through five tough rounds,
'Gainst foreign teams with funny sounds.
And then at last, the final game,
Eleven Germans are left to tame.

On Wednesday Shankly names a team,
But for one player a shattered dream.
His season's finished, blown away,
But he is still to have his say.

Rumour says they will attack,
But Netzer's playing at the back.
These Germans they can really play,
It doesn't look the Kopites' day.

The Final, postponed for a day,
Will Shankly play a different way?
In comes Toshack in place of Hall,
Now will we see the Germans fall?

Then just by chance it really pours,
Twenty-two players are on all fours.
The Referee says, 'That's enough',
Will Liverpool call the German Bluff?

The Welshman kills them in the air,
Toshack and Keegan, what a pair!!
Liverpool win the game 3-0
The Germans don't believe it still.

When I look back until this day,
I never really thought I'd play.
But then – suppose – just goes to show
In the game of football you never know!!!!

From "gosh it's Tosh". In the UEFA Cup Final from 1972-3
Liverpool met Borussia Moenchenlagbach. Originally
Toshack was not selected, but due to a freak storm the
match was abandoned. The following day Toshack heard
he had been selected only an hour before the kick-off.

Golo plays for the greatest soccer team in the Universe.
They are so mighty that their opponents never venture out of
        their own penalty area.
They are so all-conquering that Golo never touches the ball during
        a match, and very seldom sees it.
Every game seems to last a lifetime to Golo, the Gloomy Goalkeeper.

GOLO, THE
GLOOMY GOALKEEPER

Adrian Mitchell

Golo scratches white paint off the goalposts' surface to reveal the
        silver shining underneath.
He kisses the silver of the goalpost.
It does not respond.

Golo counts the small stones in the penalty area.
There are three hundred and seventy eight, which is not his lucky number.
Golo pretends to have the hiccups, then says to himself, imitating
        his sister's voice:
Don't breathe, and just die basically.

Golo breaks eight small sticks in half.
Then he has sixteen very small sticks.
He plants geranium seeds along the goal-line.
He paints a picture of a banana and sells it to the referee at half-time.

Golo finds, among the bootmarks in the dust, the print of one
        stiletto heel.
He crawls around on all fours doing lion imitations.
He tries to read his future in the palm of his hand, but forgets to
        take his glove off.
He writes a great poem about butterflies but tears it up because
        he can't think of a rhyme for Wednesday.
He knits a sweater for the camel in the Zoo.

Golo suddenly realises he can't remember if he is a man or a women.
He takes a quick look, but still can't decide.
Golo makes up his mind that grass is his favourite colour.
He puts on boots, track-suit, gloves and hat all the same colour as grass.
He paints his face a gentle shade of green.

Golo lies down on the pitch and becomes invisible.
The grass tickles the back of his neck.
At last Golo is happy.
He has fallen in love with the grass.
And the grass has fallen in love with Golo, the Gloomy Goalkeeper.

FOOTBALL

Li Yu (Chinese philosopher, A.D. 50 - 130)

A round ball and a square goal
Suggest the shape of the Yin and the Yang.
The ball is like a full moon,
And the two teams stand opposed;
Captains are appointed and take their places.

In the game make no allowances for relationship
And let there be no partiality.
Determination and coolness are essential
And there must not be the slightest irritation for failure.

Such is this game. Let its principles apply to life.

"Kemari" a Japanese ceremonial football game derived from ancient Chinese football.
19th century watercolour on silk

FOOTBALL INVADES THE WORLD

>>>>>>>>>>>>>>>>>>>>>>>>>>>>>>>>

SO WHO, EXACTLY, CAN LEGITIMATELY

CLAIM THAT THEY INVENTED FOOTBALL.

CERTAINLY NOT ANY ONE INDIVIDUAL

PERSON, BUT WHAT ABOUT ONE

PARTICULAR COUNTRY? IT HAS BEEN

SAID FREQUENTLY THAT IT'S BRITAIN

WHO LIKES TO THINK IT GAVE

SOCCER TO THE WORLD.

>>>>>>>>>>>>>>>>>>>>>>>>>>>>>>>>>

To a certain extent there's truth in that remark. A form of football, as we know from this anthology, was being played in ancient China and there's evidence that the early Greeks liked a good old kickabout: but no one nurtured the game like the British.

>>>

Many amateur football players travelled the British Empire in their capacity as sailors, soldiers, and tradesmen. Most were still playing the old rough and tumble game, although some began to export the newer rules of the Football League.

>>>

Some British teams saw themselves as 'ambassadors': in 1896 Tunbridge Wells took on United Brussels during a tour of Belgium.

>>>

But South America and, in particular, the Europeans evolved soccer into a less physical, more stylish contest than the original. Given the generic difference in cultures it maybe isn't so surprising that the French and the Germans wanted their own version.

>>>

Which they then recorded in their separate languages...

>>>

DER BALL

Rainer Maria Rilke (1875 - 1926)

Du Runder, der das Warme aus zwei Händen
im Fliegen, oben, fortgiebt, sorglos wie
sein Eigenes; was in den Gegenständen
nicht bleiben kann, zu unbeschwert für sie,

zu wenig Ding und doch noch Ding genug,
um nicht aus allem draussen Aufgereihten
unsichtbar plötzlich in uns einzugleiten:
das glitt in dich, du zwischen Fall und Flug,

noch Unentschlossener: der, wenn er steigt,
als hätte er ihn mit hinaufgehoben,
den Wurf entführt und freilässt –, und sich neigt
und einhält und den Spielenden von oben
auf einmal eine neue Stelle zeigt,
sie ordnend wie zu einer Tanzfigur,

um dann, erwartet und erwünscht von allen,
rasch, einfach, kunstlos, ganz Natur,
dem Becher hoher Hände zuzufallen.

AUF DEN TOD EINES FUSSBALLSPIELERS

Friedrich Torberg

Er war ein Kind aus Favoriten
und hiess Matthias Sindelar.
Er stand auf grünem Platz inmitten,
weil er Mittelstürmer war.

Er spielte Fussball, und er wusste
vom Leben ausserdem nicht viel.
Er lebte, weil er leben musste
vom Fussballspiel fürs Fussballspiel.

Er spielte Fussball wie kein Zweiter,
er war voll Witz und Fantasie.
Er spielte lässig, leicht und heiter,
er spielte stets, er kämpfte nie.

Er warf den blonden Schopf zur Seite,
liess seinen Herrgott gütig sein,
und stürmte durch die grüne Weite
und manchmal bis ins Tor hinein.

Es jubelte die Hohe Warte,
der Prater und das Stadion,
wenn er den Gegner lächelnd narrte
und zog ihm flinken Laufs davon.

Bis eines Tages ein andrer Gegner
ihm jählings in die Quere trat,
ein fremd und furchtbar uberlegener,
vor dem's nicht Regel gab noch Rat.

Von einem einzigen harten Tritte
fand sich der Spieler Sindelar
verstossen aus des Platzes Mitte
weil das die neue Ordnung war.

Ein Weilchen stand er noch daneben,
bevor er abging und nachhaus.
Im Fussballspiel, ganz wie im Leben,
war's mit der Wiener Schule aus.

Er war gewohnt zu kombinieren,
und kombinierte manchen Tag.
Sein Ueberblick liess ihn erspüren,
dass seine Chance im Grashahn lag.

Das Tor, durch das er dann geschritten,
lag stumm und dunkel ganz und gar.
Er war ein Kind aus Favoriten
und hiess Matthias Sindelar.

FUSSBALL (FEBST ABART UND AUSARTUNG)

Joachim Ringelnatz

Der Fussballwahn ist eine Krank-
heit, aber selten, Gott sei Dank!
Ich kenne wen, der litt akut
an Fussballwahn und Fussballwut.
Sowie er einen Gegenstand
in Kugelform und ähnlich fand,
so trat er zu und stiess mit Kraft
ihn in die bunte Nachbarschaft.
Ob es ein Schwalbennest, ein Tiegel,
ein Käse, Globus oder Igel,
ein Krug, ein Schmuckwerk am Altar,
ein Kegelball, ein Kissen war,
und wem der Gegenstand gehörte,
das war etwas, was ihn nich störte.
Bald trieb er eine Schweinenblase,
bald steife Hüte durch die Strasse.
Dan wieder mit geübtem Schwung
sties er den Fuss in Pferdedung.
Mit Schwamm und Seife betrieb er Sport.
Die Lampenkuppel brach sofort.

Das Nachtgeschirr flog zielbewusst
der Tante Berta an die Brust.
Kein Abwehrmittel wollte nützen,
nicht Stacheldraht in Stiefelspitzen,
noch Puffer, aussen angebracht.
Er siegte immer, null zu acht,
und übte weiter frisch, fromm, frei
mit Totenkopf und Straussenei.
Erschreckt durch seine wilden Stösse,
gab man ihm nie Kartoffelklösse.
Selbst vor dem Podex und den Brüsten
der Frau ergfiff ihn ein Gelüsten,
was er jedoch als Mann von Stand
aus Höflichkeit meist überwand.
Dagegen gab ein Schwartenmagen
dem Fleischer Anlass zum verklagen.
Was beim Gemüsemarkt geschah,
kommt einer Schlacht bei Leipzig nah.
Da schwirrten Aepfel, Apfelsinen
durch Publikum wie wilde Bienen.
Da sah man Blutorangen, Zwetschen
an blassen Wangen sich zerquetschen.
Das Eigelb überzog die Leiber,
ein Fischkorb platzte zwischen Weiber.
Kartoffeln spritzten und Zitronen.
Man duckte sich vor den Melonen.
Dem Krautkopf folgten Kürbisschüsse.
Dann donnerten die Kokosnüsse.
Genug! Als alles dies getan,
griff unser Held zum Grössenwahn.
Schon schäkernd mit der U-Boots-Mine,
besann er sich auf die Lawine.
Doch als pompöser Fussballstösser
fand er die Erde noch viel grösser.
Er rang mit mancherlei Problemen.
Zunächst: Wie soll man Anlauf nehmen?
Dann schiffte er von dem Balkon
sich ein in einen Luftballon.

Und blieb von da an in der Lift,
verschollen. Hat sich selbst verpufft. –
Ich warne euch, ihr Brüder Jahns,
vor dem Gebrauch des Fussballwahns!

(overleaf) Detail from "Aire Libre" the cover of a Spenish language magazine, 1920's

DER BALL IST DRIN

Reinhard Umbach

Soll der Schuss ein Treffer sein,
muss der Ball ins Tor hinein.

Ob er reinrollt oder – fliegt
oder unterm Tormann liegt,
ist im Grund höchst egal;
im Gegensatz zu jener Zahl,
mit der vom Ball der Radius
noch malgenommen werden muss,
und schon rein rechtlich so zu liegen,
dass letzte Zweifel rasch verfliegen.

2 Pi macht Balls Umdrehung voll,
die er die Linie drüber soll.
So wird erst mathematisch klar,
was vorher unumstritten war.

LE ONZIÈME HOMME

André Velter

Dernier échappé du tunnel
quand il salue
l'alignement s'est déjà défait
et les clameurs
ont volé son nom

Exilé en embuscade
il tangue sur la ligne fictive
du hors-jeu
limite mouvante
Qui d'un coup d'œil ressuscite
le coup de rein

C'est après le regard en attente
le choix de l'angle d'attaque
le jaillissement
la vitessee
le souffle coupant

On dit
torrent saisi par la tempête
qu'il déborde

On dit qu'il trace au bord des marges
un écart pour ouvrir le champ

On dit que lui
le déboussolé
centre pour aimanter les têtes

On dit qu'il est dans les nuages
Icare en bout de course
et qu'il a filé sur l'aile

LES ENFANTS DU STADE

Umberto Saba

Avec leur voix de jeunes coqs
Cette voix qui sera pour toujours dans la mémoire
Celle d'amours et de chagrins irremplaçables…

A l'autre bout du terrain
Une banderole solitaire flotte sur un petit mur.
A la mi-temps, grimpés dessus, les enfants
Lançaient comme des flèches, l'un après l'autre,
Les noms idolâtrés. Je les vois encore.
Et cette image, le soir,
Ressuscite un souvenir de mon adolescence.

Odieux d'orgueil
Les joueurs défilaient à nos pieds, sous la tribune.
Ils voyaient tout
Ils ne voyaient pas les enfants.

109

Langsam ging der Fussball am Himmel auf.
Nun sah man, dass die Tribune besetzt war
Einsam stand der dicher im Tor,
Doch der Schiedsrichter Pfiff:

Günther Grass NÄCHTLICHES STADION

AbseitS

ERWARTUNGSHALTUNG

Thomas Schleiff

"Die Angst des Tormanns beim Elfmeter"
heisst ein Roman vom Handke Peter –
doch grösser ist die Angst des Schützen:
Wird mein Elfmeter wohl auch sitzen?

Der Tormann kann ganz ruhig sein:
Man wird es ihm gar leicht verzeihn,
wenn er den Elfer nicht erwischt
und nur noch aus den Maschen fischt.

Doch schiesst der Schütze knapp daneben,
wird man es ihm nur schwer vergeben.
Man denkt: Der hat doch leichtes Spiel;
warum trifft er denn nicht ins Ziel?

So hat der Schütze schlechte Karten,
weil alle es von ihm erwarten,
dass er das Ding eiskalt verwandelt.
Versagt er, wird er schlecht behandelt.

Beim Torwart geht es umgekehrt.
Wenn er den Ball flugs abgewehrt,
dann sagen alle: Wirklich toll –
das ist weit mehr, als was er soll.

GOLEADOR

Claude Vercey

Je rôde ou je règne: dans la surface qui demeure

mon jardin (ce fut écrit) à l'affût je menace: les
coups que l'on joue à fond sont rares, affaires de flair

mais je pèse autour du point des seize mètres je tourne
comme autour de son piquet la mule dont je possède la

frappe (aussi ce fut écrit) je donne le change on
m'observe je trottine en paraissant courir je ne
m'épuiserai pas en courses vaines mais je démarre

pour faire peur dans l'espoir qu'il m'accroche
et je m'effondre aussitôt méchamment le nez dans
le gazon j'aime qu'il ait confiance en lui qu'il

me dédaigne les chiens à qui l'on confie ma garde
courent de plus en plus vite jonglent frappent des deux
pieds des athletes qui me bousculent je prends

le temps de me relever je râle il suffirait
qu'il vaguement prenne pitié sur trois foulées
un dribble un crochet le cuir il ne le reverra plus

(overleaf) "Les Footballeurs" by Jean Oliver, 1974